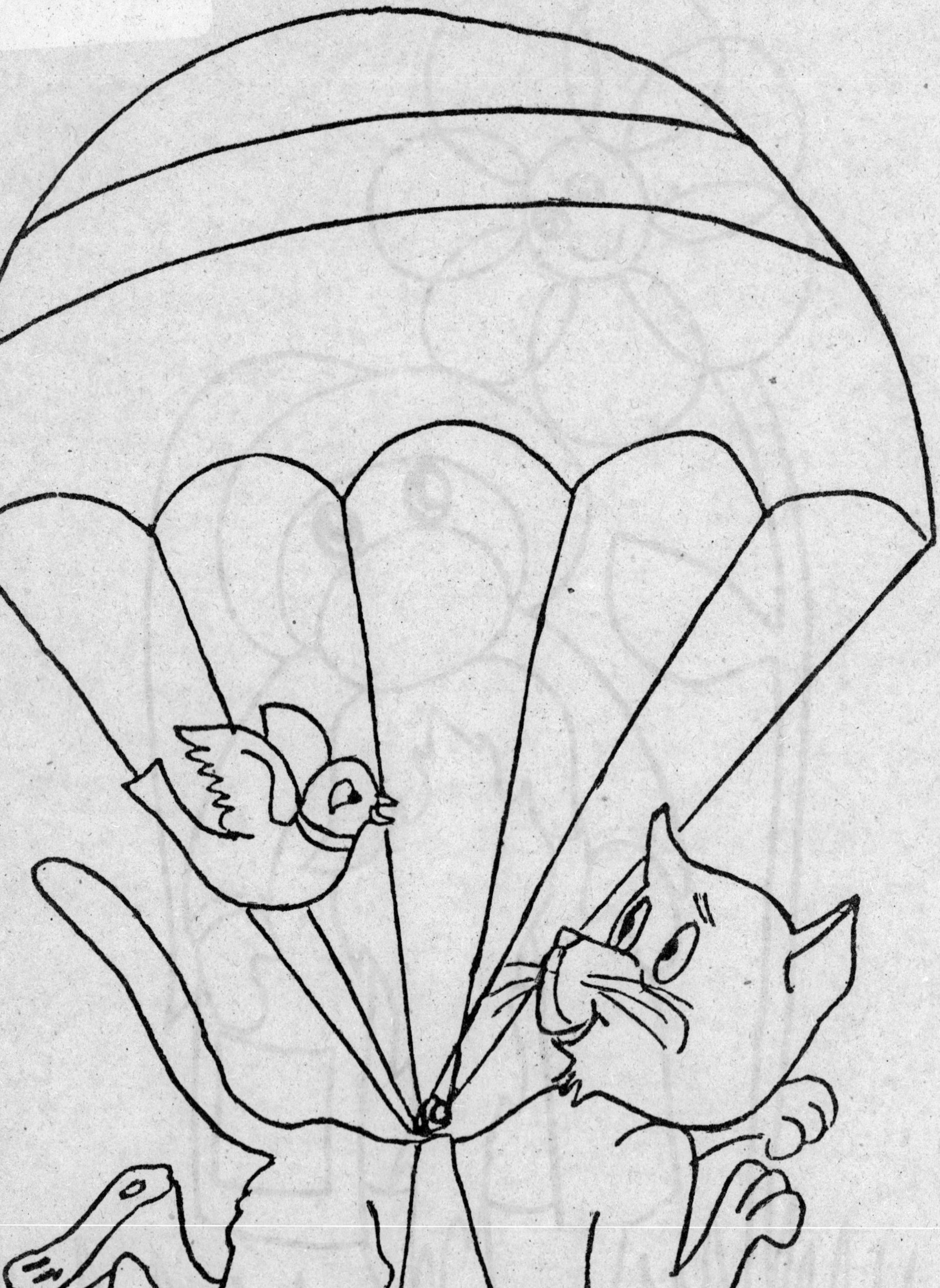

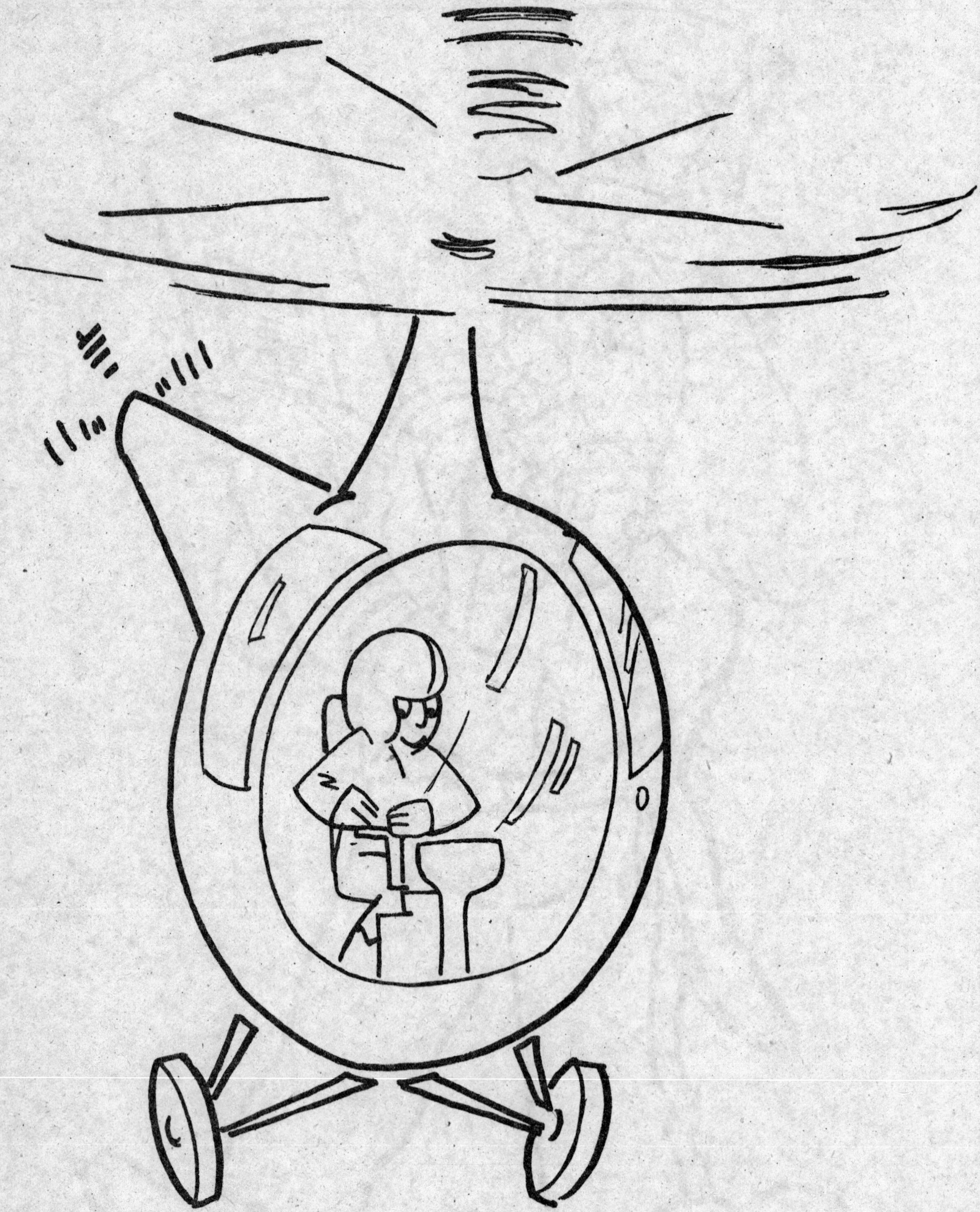

1
2

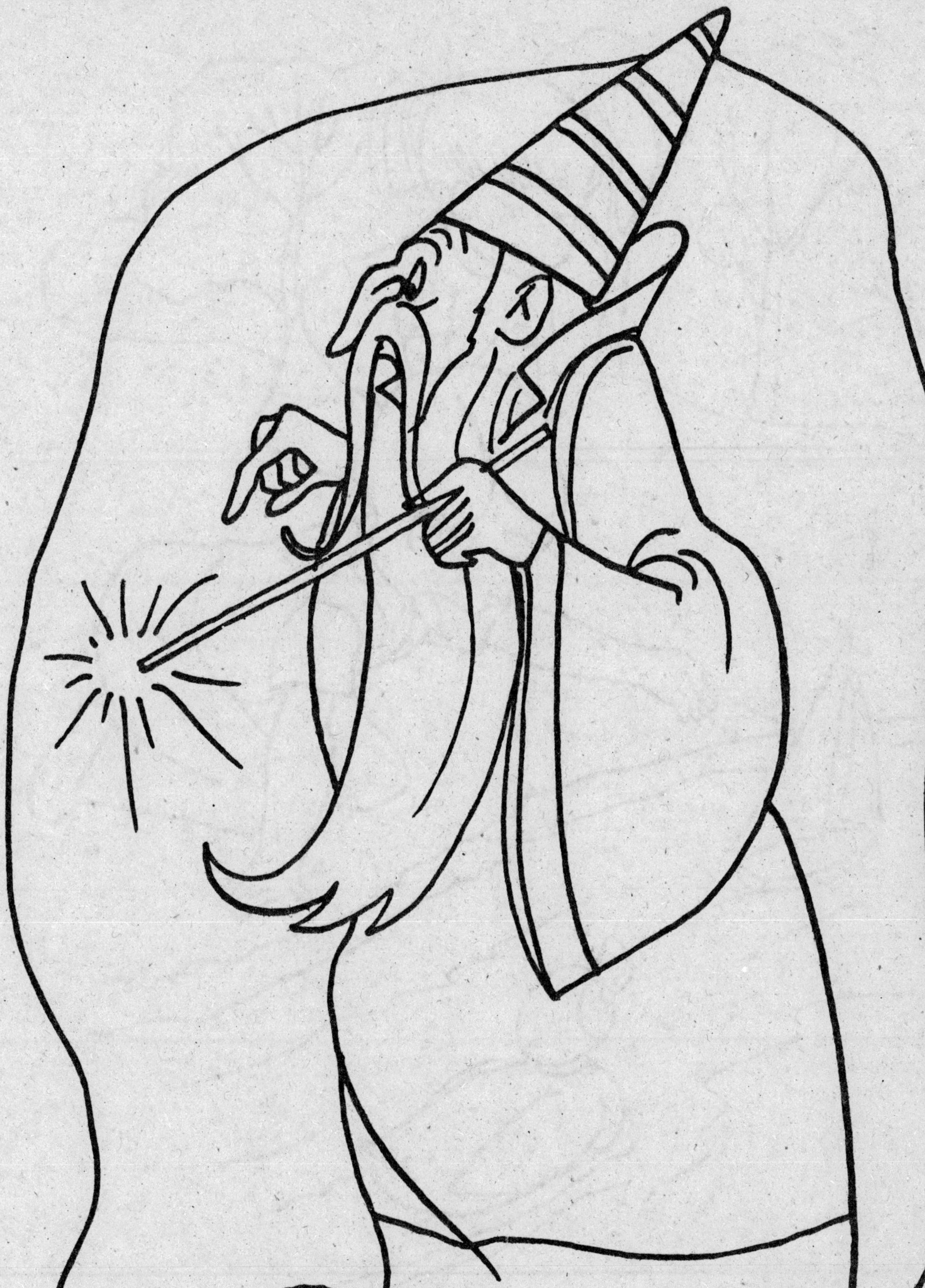

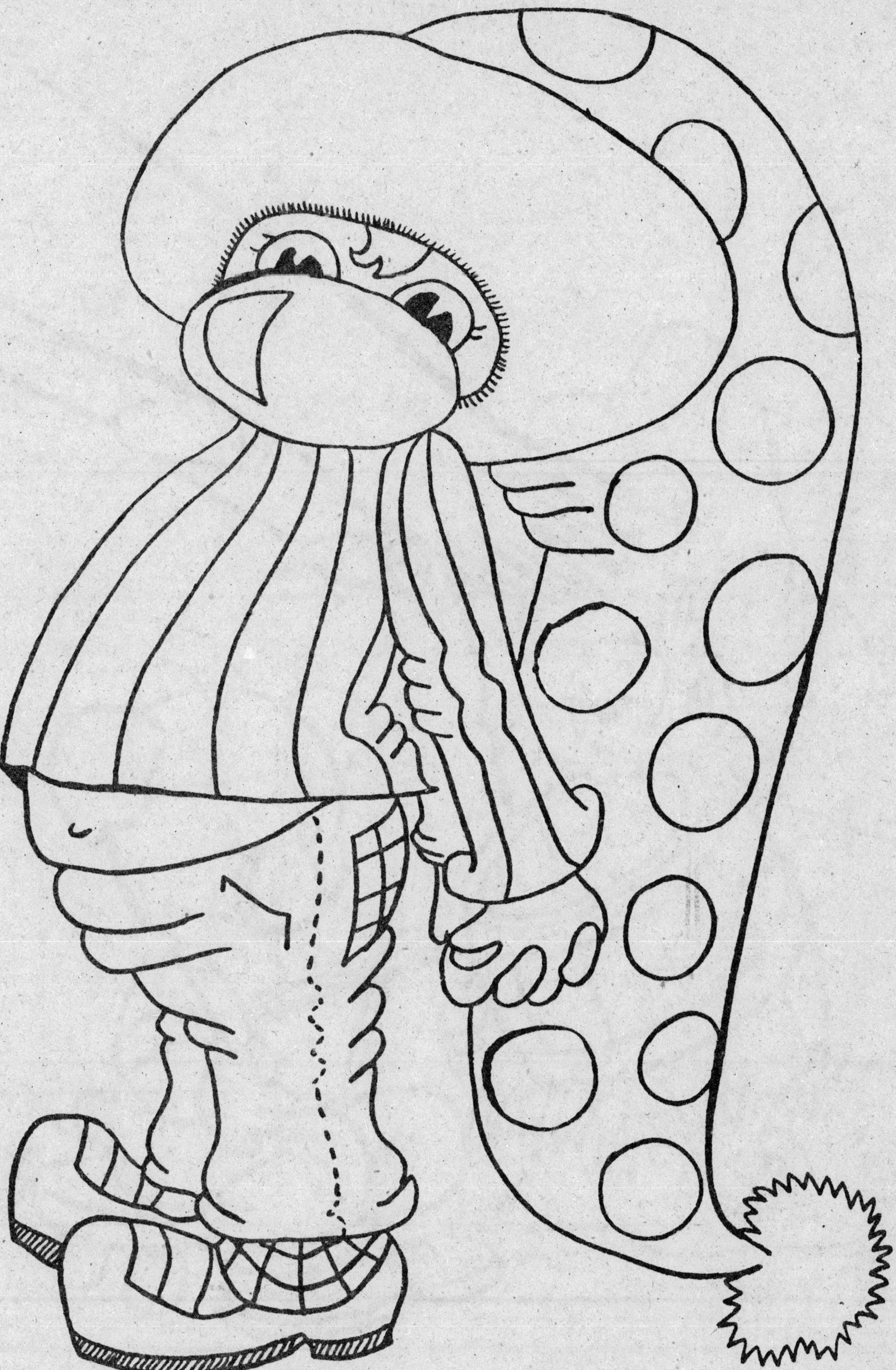

KENYA
BURMA

Gold

10

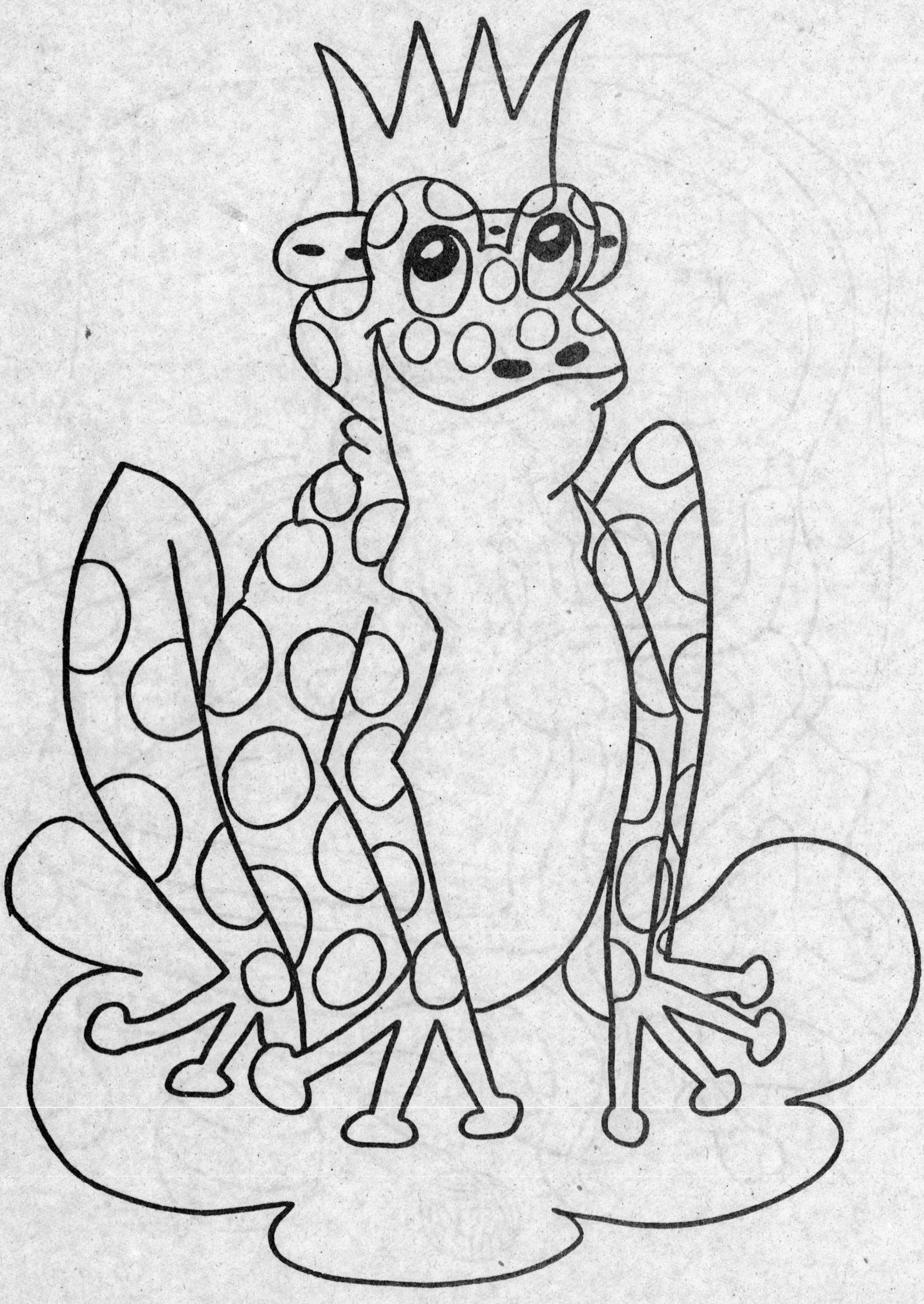

6

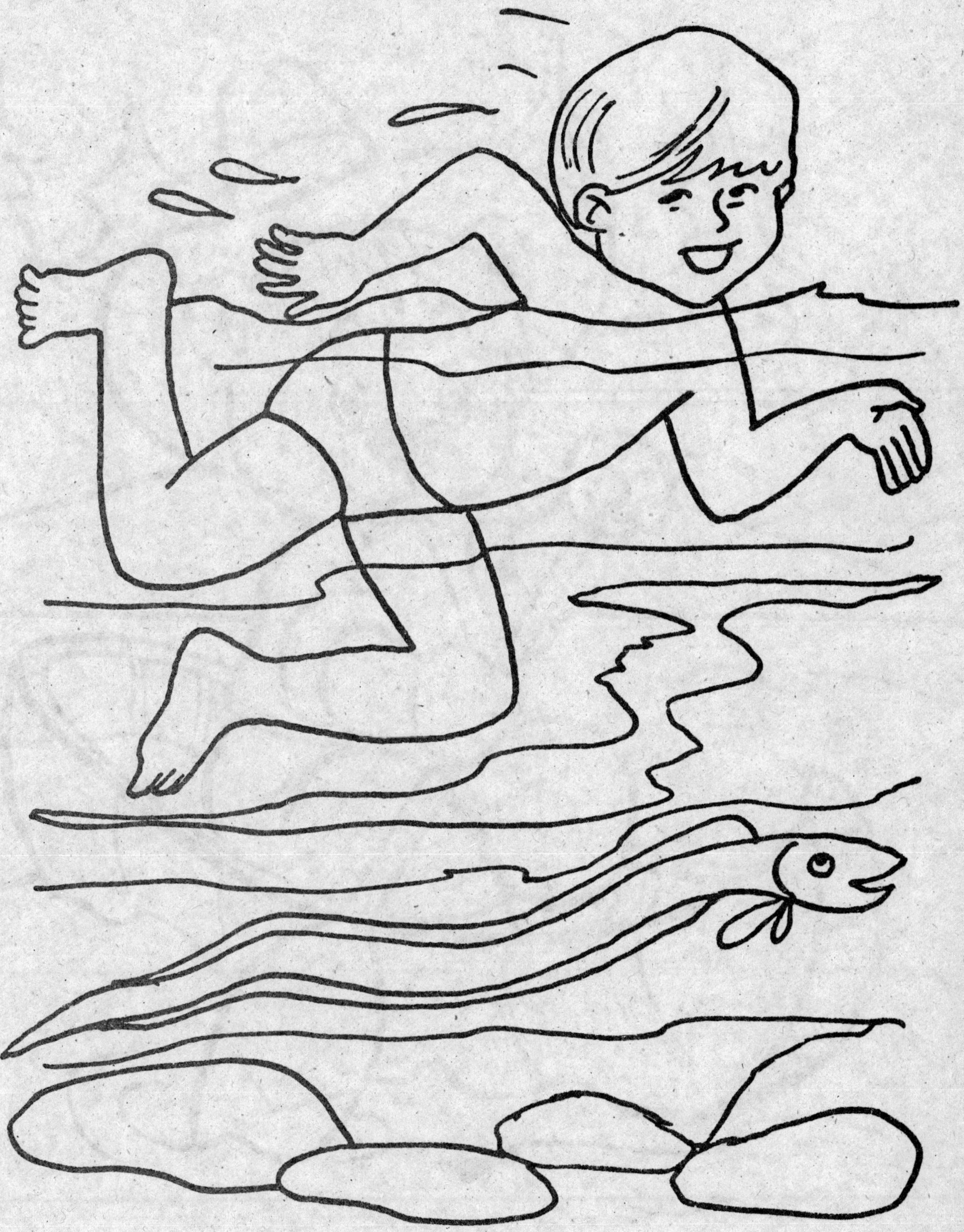

PhP PETER HADDOCK PUBLISHING
Published by
Peter Haddock Publishing,
United Kingdom YO16 6BT